PRESENTED TO:

FROM:

OCCASION:

Our purpose at Howard Publishing is to:
- Increase faith in the hearts of growing Christians
- Inspire holiness in the lives of believers
- Instill hope in the hearts of struggling people everywhere
Because He's coming again!

Who Am I? © 2004 The Forest Hills Group, LLC. All Rights Reserved
Published by Howard Publishing Co., Inc.
3117 North 7th Street, West Monroe, Louisiana 71291-2227
howardpublishing.com

Printed in Mexico

04 05 06 07 08 09 10 11 12 13   10 9 8 7 6 5 4 3 2 1

Book concept by Anderson Thomas Design, Inc.
Cover design by Jay Smith
Interior design by Matt Lehman
Cover photo by Joe McBride, Stone Stock Photography
Edited by Susan Wilson

ISBN 1-58229-352-X

Scripture quotations not otherwise marked are taken from the HOLY BIBLE, NEW INTERNATIONAL VERSION ®. Copyright © 1973, 1978, 1984 by International Bible Society. Used by permission of Zondervan. All rights reserved. Scripture quotations marked NKJV are taken from The New King James Version. Copyright © 1982 by Thomas Nelson Publishers. Used by permission. All rights reserved. Scripture quotations marked NASB are taken from the NEW AMERICAN STANDARD BIBLE®, Copyright © 1960, 1962, 1963, 1968, 1971, 1972, 1973, 1975, 1977, 1995 by The Lockman Foundation. Used by permission. Scripture quotations marked NLT are taken from the Holy Bible, New Living Translation, copyright © 1996. Used by permission of Tyndale House Publishers, Inc., Wheaton, Illinois 50189.

Italics in Scripture have been added by the author for emphasis.

WHO AM I?

MATTHEW A. PRICE & JOEL ANDERSON

POETRY
OF THE
SOUL

THE LORD YOUR GOD IS WITH YOU,
HE IS MIGHTY TO SAVE.

HE WILL TAKE
GREAT DELIGHT
IN YOU,

HE WILL QUIET YOU WITH HIS LOVE,

HE WILL REJOICE

OVER YOU

WITH SINGING.

—ZEPHANIAH 3:17

OK, HERE'S THE TRUTH: IT DOESN'T MATTER WHERE YOU'RE FROM or where you're going. It doesn't matter if you're tall or short; male or female; brown, black, or white. It doesn't matter if you're headed for the Ivies, the Big Ten, the Big 12, the SEC, the ACC, trade school, or bay one at Jiffy Lube. No matter who people think you are, no matter who you think you are, no matter who you really are, the truth—the true truth —is that deep down inside you is a desire (a longing, if you want to be honest about it) to connect to something that transcends everyone you know, everything you see, and (especially) everything you are.

Well guess what? Your quest for utter certainty and spiritual absolutes can have a happy ending. But you need to know that, despite what some people say, there is only one truth—only one path you can take that leads to total peace of mind and eternal salvation.

And how can anyone possibly know this? It's because only one faith has a Redeemer. Only one religion has a loving Creator, Jesus Christ, who gave His life so that everyone who calls on His name and believes in Him will be saved for all eternity. There are no final exams, no feats of strength, no special diets, no long hours chanting and staring at the ceiling. Just ask and believe. That's it.

Of course, as with most things that are simple, there are layers of complexity in the Christian life that a thousand lifetimes can't uncover. In fact, discovering different facets of who God is and why He created us makes Christianity a daily, moment-by-moment joy. That's why Poetry of the Soul isn't a typical guided journaling series. Sure, it's designed to help you discover who you are in God's eyes, but more importantly, it will help you grow to know Him and love Him more deeply.

There's another important point that should be made. Poetry of the Soul doesn't treat young people like, well . . . they're young. Yes, the graphics are cool, and your bookstore probably displays their copies in the youth section. But, truthfully, the whole idea of treating anyone between the ages of thirteen and nineteen as anything less than a fully functioning human being has only been an accepted viewpoint (and a rather condescending one at that) for the last fifty years or so.

Look in the Bible. Nowhere do you find special consideration given for a young person's age when it comes to their understanding of what is true and perfect and good. Nowhere is someone told, "Well, since you're only sixteen, you can't have clearly formed opinions on what's right and wrong, and so we won't hold you responsible for your actions."

Look at American history. In almost every era, with recent exceptions, there has been an age of accountability when children pass into adulthood. At that point they would be expected to help on the family farms, to bear arms to protect their communities, and to worship with their parents. While they probably enjoyed the company of other young people, they weren't shuffled off into youth groups at church, and they didn't think they should wait until after they'd graduated from college or got a full-time job to start acting responsibly. They were vital members of society and were expected to conduct themselves as such.

There is no better example of this than the way God called young people to do and believe great things in both the Old and New Testaments. As a young boy, Samuel heard God's voice and knew that he was meant for a lifetime of ministry. God chose Mary, most likely at the age of sixteen or seventeen, to be the mother of Jesus.

If God held young people in such high regard thousands of years ago, why doesn't He feel the same today? The short answer is that He does! Any person of any age who seeks God will find Him. Anyone who desires to know why they were created and what God's purpose is for their life can find out by simply and earnestly asking, seeking, and believing.

And that's the purpose behind Poetry of the Soul. It's our desire to help young people in their search for answers that pop culture and false religions are unable to provide. It's our mission to equip young people to think for themselves, to take up positions of leadership, and to set examples of godliness for their lost and confused peers.

One of the journal pages in this book has the standard "write down the names of your family and friends in case you get hit on the head and forget" questions. The rest, however, require deep and personal reflection. Before you fill in these lines, read the accompanying text; then answer the questions with wisdom and maturity.

And remember: If you're past the age of thirteen, you're a young adult. It's time to think like one, act like one, serve like one, and lead like one. We pray that Poetry of the Soul will help you clarify and affirm your convictions as you begin the exciting journey that awaits you.

WHO AM I?

Ah, the age-old question: "Who am I?" And, of course, there are its "first cousins": "Does God really love me?" and "What effect is my life having on the lives of my friends?" and "What will happen to me when I die?" and "Why do I have to study chemistry when it has nothing to do with how bad my hair looks today?" Yes, some things can't be answered with a simple nod, shrug, or wistful sigh. They require personal reflection. And time.

As a believer in the one true God, questions like this also require your prayerful consideration (well, maybe not the hair thing—but otherwise, definitely). As you fill in the pages of *Who Am I?* remember that you're keeping a journal of how you feel about your faith, your family, your friends, and yourself at this exact point in your life. Someday, many years from now, you'll want to read these pages again to see how your perspectives and attitudes have changed. Believe me, you don't want the you then to say about the you now, "Would it have killed me to put a little more thought into this? I mean, c'mon!"

Seriously. Give it your best shot. There's no doubt whatsoever that you're worth the effort!

My name _____

My birth date _____

My birthplace _____

My parents' names _____

My siblings' names _____

My maternal grandparents' names _____

My paternal grandparents' names _____

My pet's name _____

My school _____

My best friend at school _____

My favorite subject _____

My favorite teacher _____

My church _____

My best friend at church _____

My favorite Bible verse _____

My favorite food _____

My favorite color _____

My style _____

My favorite book _____

My favorite song _____

My favorite movie _____

My favorite television show _____

My favorite hangout _____

My favorite sport _____

THE BLACK & WHITE STUFF

WHO AM I IN THE BIG PICTURE?
HOW DO I FIT INTO THE SCHEME OF HISTORY?

Why am I here on this planet,

in this particular time in history,

as a citizen of this country,

as a member of my community,

as a child of my parents,

as a big or little brother or sister,

as a student at my school,

as a friend or acquaintance of someone special,

and as a part of God's creation?

I am here right now because God has a big plan for eternity, and I am a part of it! My purpose in this short life is to get to know God, walk with Him daily, and allow Him to unfold His plan for my life. When I see where He is at work within me, I need to have the faith to become a part of that work.

Everything I do today has an impact on my eternal life. This life lasts only fifty, seventy, or maybe one hundred years, but eternity—it never ends! So, as long as I'm here, I am on a life-long journey of discovery, finding out about who I am, why I am here, who God is, why He put me here, and how I can play an important role in His plan.

This means that God is active in my life at all times. Romans 8:28 NASB says that "God causes *all things* to work together for good." But you gotta hear *who* this promise goes out to: "those who love God, to those who are called according to *His* purpose." This doesn't say that God *causes* all things, but that He ultimately causes all things to *work together for good.* Everything, even seemingly tragic things, are all part of a big plan that, depending on my faith and attitude, can be used to shape me into the eternal being God wants me to become.

"Lord, guide me as I read and write in this book. Please help me to see how I fit into Your big plan. Give me the courage and the faith to play my part, even if it is difficult. Amen."

I am a son or a daughter.

THINK ABOUT IT

What qualities do you see and admire in your parents' lives? What traits of theirs do you hope to avoid? Why do you think God placed you in your family?

READ ABOUT IT

"Honor your father and your mother, that your days may be long upon the land which the LORD your God is giving you." (Exodus 20:12 NKJV)

Even though you and your parents don't see eye to eye on everything, they really do have a lot of great qualities. You may not tell them very often; but you love them, and you're very thankful that they're your parents.

THE WORLD'S FIRST PARENTS

They were the father and mother of the entire human race. They also, through their disobedience, brought sin into the world. Unlike Adam and Eve, we should never try to hide our sins from God but should, rather, confess and ask for forgiveness. Read about Adam and Eve in Genesis 1–5.

WRITE ABOUT IT

What characteristics do you see in your parents that you'd like to **attain** in your own life? Are there any you'd like to **avoid**?

I am more than what people think I am.

THINK ABOUT IT

When others see you, what is their first impression?
What would surprise people about you if they could read your mind?

READ ABOUT IT

"Don't be concerned about the outward beauty that depends on fancy hairstyles, expensive jewelry, or beautiful clothes. You should be known for the beauty that comes from within, the unfading beauty of a gentle and quiet spirit, which is so precious to God." (1 Peter 3:3–4 NLT)

DON'T JUDGE A BOOK BY ITS COVER

"The LORD said to Samuel, 'Do not consider his appearance or his height, for I have rejected him. The LORD does not look at the things man looks at. Man looks at the outward appearance, but the LORD looks at the heart.'" (1 Samuel 16:7)

God told the prophet Samuel to anoint a new king for Israel. So Samuel went to the home of Jesse and asked to see his sons. When he saw the oldest (who was tall and handsome), he thought to himself, "Surely this is the one." But God told him to keep looking. After meeting the seven sons Jesse presented, Samuel asked if there was anyone else. David was the youngest and least important of Jesse's eight sons. He wasn't even invited to the meeting! But God showed everyone that David was much more than anyone could see on the outside.

Read the whole story in 1 Samuel 16:1–13.

OK, so you have a highly evolved sense of style and everyone wants to know where you bought your new shoes. But, hey, you're more than all that. God dwells within your heart, and He has changed you in ways that others don't see.

WRITE ABOUT IT

What would others say about you after first meeting you?
What are you trying to convey to others by the words you use and the way you dress?

I am created in the image of God.

THINK ABOUT IT

If you are made in the image of God, what are some of the qualities you and God have in common?

READ ABOUT IT

"Thank you for making me so wonderfully complex! Your workmanship is marvelous—and how well I know it." (Psalm 139:14 NLT)

"So God created people in his own image; God patterned them after himself; male and female he created them." (Genesis 1:27 NLT)

You may not like how you talk. You may not like your nose or your ears or your mouth. You may not like how you move your arms when you walk. But don't ever forget that you were created in the image of the infinite, boundless, all-knowing, all-powerful Creator of the universe. So maybe you're not so bad after all, huh? In fact, maybe you're perfect just the way you are.

WHAT IS GOD LIKE? Well, until we get to heaven, we will only be able to "see" Him through the Bible and His creation. In Genesis, He shows us that He is creative, He is loving, He enjoys beauty, He loves companionship, He delights in the beauty and diversity of stars, planets, plants, people, and animals. He also reveals that He is holy and desires that we be holy. In the Old Testament, God shows us that He is just, yet merciful. He provides for His own, He answers prayer, and He disciplines and protects His chosen ones while He judges and punishes the unrighteous. In the New Testament, God showed His love for all of humanity by sending Jesus, His Son, to live among us, die for us, rise again to defeat sin and death, and ascend into heaven to prepare a place for us.

WRITE ABOUT IT

How can you reflect the image of God in the way you look?

_____

_____

_____

_____

How can you reflect the image of God in the way you think?

_____

_____

_____

_____

_____

How can you reflect the image of God in the way you act?

_____

_____

_____

_____

_____

Psalm 139 is a great one to read and ponder when it comes to the question of "Who am I?" In this powerful meditation, King David reflects on how God knew us before we were even born, how He protects us, how He is everywhere at all times, and how precious it is to know Him and be known by Him.

PSALM 139

1 O Lord, you have searched me and you know me.
2 You know when I sit and when I rise;
   you perceive my thoughts from afar.
3 You discern my going out and my lying down;
   you are familiar with all my ways.
4 Before a word is on my tongue
   you know it completely, O Lord.

5 You hem me in—behind and before;
   you have laid your hand upon me.
6 Such knowledge is too wonderful for me,
   too lofty for me to attain.

7 Where can I go from your Spirit?
   Where can I flee from your presence?
8 If I go up to the heavens, you are there;
   if I make my bed in the depths, you are there.
9 If I rise on the wings of the dawn,
   if I settle on the far side of the sea,
10 even there your hand will guide me,
   your right hand will hold me fast.

11 If I say, "Surely the darkness will hide me
   and the light become night around me,"
12 even the darkness will not be dark to you;
   the night will shine like the day,
   for darkness is as light to you.

13 For you created my inmost being;
   you knit me together in my mother's womb.
14 I praise you because I am fearfully and wonderfully made;
   your works are wonderful, I know that full well.
15 My frame was not hidden from you
   when I was made in the secret place.
   When I was woven together in the depths of the earth,
16 your eyes saw my unformed body.
   All the days ordained for me were written in your book
   before one of them came to be.

SEARCH ME, O GOD, AND KNOW MY hEART; TEST ME ANd KNOW MY aNXIOUS THOUGHTS.

17 How precious to me are your thoughts, O God!
   How vast is the sum of them!
18 Were I to count them,
   they would outnumber the grains of sand.
   When I awake, I am still with you.

23 Search me, O God, and know my heart;
   test me and know my anxious thoughts.
24 See if there is any offensive way in me,
   and lead me in the way everlasting.

WRITE ABOUT **PSALM 139**

verse 1 *O LORD, you have searched me and you know me.*
Describe how it feels to know God can see deep into your soul and know everything about you.

_____

_____

_____

verse 4 *Before a word is on my tongue you know it completely, O LORD.*
Should this make you comfortable or uneasy? Why or why not?

_____

_____

_____

_____

verse 5 *You hem me in—behind and before; you have laid your hand upon me.*
Name times when you were glad you had boundaries.

_____

_____

_____

_____

verse 14 *I praise you because I am fearfully and wonderfully made.*
What are some marvelous things about how God made you?

_____

_____

_____

verse 16 *All the days ordained for me were written in your book before one of them came to be.*
If God knew about all of your days before you ever lived one of them, then He also knows when your last day on this earth will be. How can this knowledge help you to be less fearful of death?

_____

_____

_____

_____

verse 23 *Search me, O God, and know my heart; test me and know my anxious thoughts.*
What are you worried about? Make a list of things that bother you or make you worry.

_____

_____

_____

_____

_____

_____

_____

verse 24 *See if there is any offensive way in me, and lead me in the way everlasting.*
Are there some bad attitudes you need to deal with? Are you refusing to forgive someone?
Do you really want God to "lead you in the the way everlasting" (a life of obedience to His ways)?

_____

_____

_____

_____

WHO AM I?

I am God's child, intimately known by Him.

THINK ABOUT IT

How well do others know you? How much of yourself do you share with those who care about you most? How intimate is your relationship with Him?

READ ABOUT IT

"O Lord, you have examined my heart and know everything about me." (Psalm 139:1 NLT)

"Even the very hairs of your head are all numbered." (Matthew 10:30)

Psychologists say that it often takes years to honestly evaluate yourself and that you may discover many things you won't like in the process. Here's a little advice: Ignore the experts. God loves you for who you are and so should you.

Does it make you nervous to think that God knows everything about you, even the stuff that you would never EVER tell another living soul? NEWS FLASH: Your heavenly Father already sees right into the deepest, most hidden corners of your soul—after all, He made you! Imagine this—He knows all your secret sins, yet He still loves you and calls you His own. He even longs for you to know Him as deeply as He knows you! Does this mean that He doesn't mind if you are hiding secret sins? God is holy (totally pure), so the cleaner you are, the closer you can be to Him. Ask Him to help you repent of any sin in your life, so you can be closer to Him.

> **GOD LOVED YOU BEFORE YOU COULD EVER DO ANYTHING TO EARN HIS LOVE. JESUS PROVED IT.**
>
> "Now, no one is likely to die for a good person, though someone might be willing to die for a person who is especially good. But God showed his great love for us by sending Christ to die for us while we were still sinners. And since we have been made right in God's sight by the blood of Christ, he will certainly save us from God's judgment."
> (Romans 5:7–9 NLT)

WRITE ABOUT IT

Intimacy comes by deeply knowing and being known by someone. Write about the ways you have grown in intimacy with someone you really care about.

Name of special person:

How do you communicate?

How do you spend time together?

What common interests do you share?

What do you confide in each other?

How do you show your affection for each other?

You can be intimate with God in many of the same ways you have just listed. Communicate honestly with God, spend time with Him, show Him affection, share with God your secret joys, hopes, goals, fears, doubts, and sins. This will bring new levels of intimacy you've never known!

WHO AM I?

I am a mosaic of experiences.

THINK ABOUT IT

What are some of your most vivid memories?
Why are these experiences so important?

READ ABOUT IT

"I recall all you have done, O Lᴏʀᴅ; I remember your wonderful deeds of long ago." (Psalm 77:11 ɴʟᴛ)

Your life has been marked by a series of events, experiences, and relationships that have helped shape you into the person you are today. Some events have been difficult, others delightful. Many of these milestones are infinitely important—like the day you received Jesus as your Savior. Others are far more ordinary. But each one, when added to the next, has made you the person you are today.

THE EXPERIENCES OF PAUL:

"Five different times the Jews gave me thirty-nine lashes. Three times I was beaten with rods. Once I was stoned. Three times I was shipwrecked. Once I spent a whole night and a day adrift at sea. I have traveled many weary miles. I have faced danger from flooded rivers and from robbers. I have faced danger from my own people, the Jews, as well as from the Gentiles. I have faced danger in the cities, in the deserts, and on the stormy seas. . . . Often I have been hungry and thirsty and have gone without food. Often I have shivered with cold, without enough clothing to keep me warm." (2 Corinthians 11:24–27 ɴʟᴛ)

WRITE ABOUT IT

How have you seen God take care of you over the years? Recall a situation when God was protecting or guiding you.

WHO AM I IN CHRIST? HOW HAS THE LIFE, DEATH, AND RESURRECTION OF JESUS MADE A DIFFERENCE IN WHO I AM?

If _____ [my name] is in Christ, he/she is a new creation; the old has gone, the new has come! 2 Corinthians 5:17

Now he [God] has reconciled _____ [my name] by Christ's physical body through death to present him/her holy in his sight, without blemish and free from accusation. Colossians 1:22

How great is the love the Father has lavished on us, that _____ [my name] should be called a child of God! And that is what we are! 1 John 3:1

There is now no condemnation for _____ [my name] who is in Christ Jesus. Romans 8:1

The LORD your God is with you, _____ [my name], he is mighty to save. He will take great delight in you, He will quiet you with his love, he will rejoice over you with singing. Zephaniah 3:17

In Christ I am a new creation. I am reconciled (made right) with God. I am now a child of God. I will not face condemnation for my sins and mistakes. I am one whom God delights in. I have a new identity—I am a Christian! My identity is not found in how I dress, what kind of music I like, whether or not I am athletic, smart, good-looking, or popular. As a Christian my identity is found in Christ. I am to live as He lived, learn to act like He acted, treat others the way He treated people. Jesus didn't care what others thought of Him. He wasn't interested in being liked or fitting in. He listened to His heavenly Father and obeyed Him, even when it meant giving His life away.

Some people loved Jesus. Many hated Him. But even 2000 years later, nobody can deny that He changed the course of human history because of His strength, love, compassion, example, and sacrifice. Instead of placing your identity in a label such as jock, brain, prom queen, class clown, goth, punk, metal head, or geek; proudly proclaim your identity as a follower of Christ.

"Lord, help me to learn as much as I can about who Jesus is, so I can strive to become more like Him. Let me never be ashamed to claim my identity as a follower of Christ. Amen."

WHO AM I?

I am blessed.

THINK ABOUT IT

What five things are you
most thankful for?

READ ABOUT IT

**"No matter what happens, always be thankful, for this is God's will for
you who belong to Christ Jesus." (1 Thessalonians 5:18 NLT)**

Doctors and nurses who treat elderly patients typically say that a good attitude and a thankful
heart are the two basic keys to a long and productive life. This makes perfect sense. Everyone,
regardless of their age, feels better and happier when they're at peace with their lives and are
happy with what God has given them.

JOSEPH'S BLESSING IN DISGUISE

Joseph was a man of great integrity. Even when he faced temptations and life or death
situations, Joseph did what was right because he loved God. God blessed Joseph's faithfulness and made him a powerful leader over one of history's greatest civilizations. You
may not rule a nation one day, but by letting God rule your heart you can be assured
that your future will be very bright. Read about Joseph in Genesis chapters 30–50.

WRITE ABOUT IT   List at least ten things for which you are thankful.

1. _____

_____

2. _____

_____

3. _____

_____

4. _____

_____

5. _____

_____

6. _____

_____

7. _____

_____

8. _____

_____

9. _____

_____

10. _____

_____

I am forgiven.

THINK ABOUT IT

What is the biggest mistake you made during the past year? What did you learn from this mistake?

READ ABOUT IT

"If we confess our sins, he is faithful and just and will forgive us our sins and purify us from all unrighteousness." (1 John 1:9)

"We all make many mistakes, but those who control their tongues can also control themselves in every other way." (James 3:2 NLT)

Everyone makes mistakes. Lots of them. Sometimes mistakes can be very serious, and there's no way to correct their consequences. More often a mistake becomes a difficult, but ultimately rewarding, learning experience. In any event, don't compound the situation you've created by trying to talk your way out of it or by blaming others. Only God can turn foolishness into wisdom. Only God will completely forgive you for your poor decisions and restore you to wholeness. All you have to do is ask.

DAVID'S MISTAKE

He was the greatest king in Israel's history, and he was an ancestor of Jesus through Joseph's lineage. Yet David committed terrible sins in his life. One of the worst was arranging for the death of a man named Uriah so he could marry Uriah's wife, Bathsheba. David's life was redeemed by his willingness to confess his sins and earnestly seek forgiveness. Remember that God is willing to forgive you no matter what you've done. Read about David in 1 Samuel 16–1 Kings 2.

WRITE ABOUT IT

A good definition of sin is "to miss the mark." In what ways have you missed the mark of God's holiness and perfect love?

I am a friend.

THINK ABOUT IT

What qualities do you want to see in another person before you establish a close friendship? Do you possess these qualities? Do the friends you have right now have these qualities?

READ ABOUT IT

"A friend is always loyal." (Proverbs 17:17 NLT)

There's an old saying that the only way to have a friend is to be one. The truth of this lies in the fact that friendship is not a relationship based on temporary or purely selfish needs. It's based on the mutual respect, concern, and warmth two people feel for one another. If you know someone who's nice to you because you're helping them with their homework or because they want a ride to school each morning, then it's difficult to say exactly what your relationship is, but it's easy to see that it's not a friendship. Be discerning. When you have a lot, your "friends" will know you; when you don't have anything, then you'll know your friends.

BEST FRIENDS

"After David had finished talking with Saul, Jonathan became one in spirit with David, and he loved him as himself. From that day Saul kept David with him and did not let him return to his father's house. And Jonathan made a covenant with David because he loved him as himself. Jonathan took off the robe he was wearing and gave it to David, along with his tunic, and even his sword, his bow and his belt." (1 Samuel 18:1–4)

David and Jonathan were best friends. Nothing in the world—not even death—would be able to break the bonds of their deep friendship. Read all about them in 1 Samuel chapters 18–20.

WRITE ABOUT IT

List five qualities you look for in a friend.
Do you have these same qualities?

1 The LORD is my shepherd, I shall not be in want.
2 He makes me lie down in green pastures,
  he leads me beside quiet waters,
3 he restores my soul.
  He guides me in paths of righteousness
  for his name's sake.
4 Even though I walk
  through the valley of the shadow of death,
  I will fear no evil,
  for you are with me;
  your rod and your staff,
  they comfort me.

5 You prepare a table before me
  in the presence of my enemies.
  You anoint my head with oil;
  my cup overflows.
6 Surely goodness and love will follow me
  all the days of my life,
  and I will dwell in the house
  of the LORD forever.

SURELY goODNESS AND LOVE
WILL fOLLOW ME ALL THE DAYS Of My LIFE

PERSONAL PSALM

Read Psalm 23 and see how David expressed his relationship with God. Next, think about how you might write your own psalm of praise. Use this as a starting point for your personal expression, then write your own on the following pages.

The LORD is my ☐ Pilot ☐ Guardian ☐ King ☐ Coach ☐ Parent.
He lovingly provides everything I need.
He ☐ watches over me ☐ prepares me for action ☐ trains me ☐ guides me
because He loves me so much and cares for me so dearly.
He ☐ comforts me ☐ protects me ☐ assures me ☐ blesses me
because I belong to Him, and because He desires to show Himself to me.
Even though ☐ life is hard ☐ I feel like I am all alone ☐ I am confused
☐ I have doubts ☐ I am afraid of _____ ,
I will not despair or tremble in fear, for He is with me.
LORD, Your ☐ Word ☐ love ☐ mercy ☐ grace ☐ commands ☐ salvation
comforts me, guides me, and keeps me from wandering off and losing myself.
You prepare a lavish feast for me, proving Your love through
☐ answered prayers ☐ fellowship with other believers ☐ Your Word.
You protect me and take my side even in the presence of
☐ my enemies ☐ those who don't understand me ☐ those who exclude me
☐ those who wish to harm me ☐ those who_____.
You honor me and show me I am so valuable to You by giving me
☐ beautiful sunsets ☐ nature ☐ good health ☐ eternal life ☐ a bright future.
My life is full to overflowing! I know that Your goodness and mercy will cover me all
the days of my life. I live each day with Your presence, but it is such a joy to know that
I will also live with You forever in heaven!

YOUR PSALM

As you begin to write your psalm, keep in mind a few things. This is a great opportunity for you to be completely honest before God. No emotion is unsafe when talking to Him. He wants to hear about everything; you can praise Him or ask Him questions. The key is simply bringing your heart before His heart.

OUR SOUL WAITS FOR THE LORD; HE IS OUR HELP AND OUR SHIELD. FOR OUR HEART REJOICES IN HIM, BECAUSE WE TRUST IN HIS HOLY NAME.

—PSALM 33:20–21 NASB

WHO AM I?

I am both a leader and a follower.

THINK ABOUT IT

Who looks up to you and follows your lead? What kind of leader are you?
Whom do you look up to and follow? What kind of leaders are they?

READ ABOUT IT

"If God has given you leadership ability, take the responsibility seriously. And if you have a gift for showing kindness to others, do it gladly."
(Romans 12:8 NLT)

Leadership, at best, is an inexact science. Perhaps that's why people politely call it an "art." If you mess up a painting it's probably not going to ruin someone's life. But leadership is all about real life because everyone at some point is a leader and everyone always follows in the footsteps of others. There is only one person who has ever lived whose life and words ring consistently true: Jesus Christ. By following His words and example, you will not only be a better leader, you will also know who you should and shouldn't follow.

FOLLOWER TURNED LEADER

While still a small boy, he was called by God to serve as a judge over Israel. Samuel helped with small duties early in his life as he assisted the high priest, Eli, in the tabernacle. His character was so admired that he eventually became one of the most important judges in Israel's history. Samuel's life is an example of why it's important to take life seriously while you're young so that others will trust you with more important responsibilities as you grow older. Read about Samuel in 1 Samuel chapters 1–28.

WRITE ABOUT IT

How does seeing hypocrites in leadership positions make you feel about being a follower? Name some ways you can assert a positive influence without being considered self-righteous.

WHO AM I?

I am a work in progress.

THINK ABOUT IT

Being young doesn't mean you don't have great things to offer the kingdom of God.
Do you feel like older people respect your opinions and insights?

READ ABOUT IT

"Don't let anyone look down on you because you are young, but set an example for the believers in speech, in life, in love, in faith and in purity." (1 Timothy 4:12)

Time, distance, and perspective. These are not just properties for a geometric theorem. They are also components of the maturing process. Believe it or not, in a few years many of the concerns, relationships, and preferences that are so important today will be long forgotten or, at the very least, won't seem like such a big deal after all. That's why you should always take an eternal perspective. Pray that God will show you what is truly significant and lasting and that He will give you wisdom that transcends the cares of the moment.

WHO WAS TIMOTHY?

He was a timid young man who sometimes was not taken seriously because of his age. But Timothy was also the trusted companion of Paul and was sent by Paul as his representative to the troubled church in Corinth. Although Timothy was apparently unsuccessful, Paul still believed in him and left him in Ephesus to build the church in that great city. Remember Timothy's life if you don't succeed at something important. Never give up, because it's an absolute certainty that God will never give up on you. Read about Timothy in 1st and 2nd Timothy.

WRITE ABOUT IT

What milestones of progress have you reached so far in your life?

_____

_____

_____

_____

_____

_____

_____

_____

_____

_____

_____

_____

_____

_____

_____

_____

_____

_____

_____

LOOKING CLOSER

WHO AM I AMONG GOD'S SERVANTS? HOW HAVE I BEEN UNIQUELY GIFTED TO WORK IN GOD'S KINGDOM?

"The Kingdom of Heaven can be illustrated by the story of a man going on a trip. He called together his servants and gave them money to invest for him while he was gone. He gave five bags of gold to one, two bags of gold to another, and one bag of gold to the last—dividing it in proportion to their abilities—and then left on his trip. The servant who received the five bags of gold began immediately to invest the money and soon doubled it. The servant with two bags of gold also went right to work and doubled the money. But the servant who received the one bag of gold dug a hole in the ground and hid the master's money for safekeeping.

"After a long time their master returned from his trip and called them to give an account of how they had used his money. The servant to whom he had entrusted the five bags of gold said, 'Sir, you gave me five bags of gold to invest, and I have doubled the amount.' The master was full of praise. 'Well done, my good and faithful servant. You have been faithful in handling this small amount, so now I will give you many more responsibilities. Let's celebrate together!'

"Next came the servant who had received the two bags of gold, with the report, 'Sir, you gave me two bags of gold to invest, and I have doubled the amount.' The master said, 'Well done, my good and faithful servant. You have been faithful in handling this small amount, so now I will give you many more responsibilities. Let's celebrate together!'

"Then the servant with the one bag of gold came and said, 'Sir, I know you are a hard man, harvesting crops you didn't plant and gathering crops you didn't cultivate. I was afraid I would lose your money, so I hid it in the earth and here it is.'

"But the master replied, 'You wicked and lazy servant! You think I'm a hard man, do you, harvesting crops I didn't plant and gathering crops I didn't cultivate? Well, you should at least have put my money into the bank so I could have some interest. Take the money from this servant and give it to the one with the ten bags of gold. To those who use well what they are given, even more will be given, and they will have an abundance. But from those who are unfaithful, even what little they have will be taken away. Now throw this useless servant into outer darkness, where there will be weeping and gnashing of teeth.' "

(Matthew 25:14–30 NLT)

As a servant of my Master, nothing I have is actually mine.
My time, my money,
my talents, my energy,
my friendships, my future,
my dreams, my whole life—
all of these gifts are on loan from God, my Master.
He didn't give them to me to use selfishly—He LENT them to me to do His work during my lifetime—to praise Him and to point others to Him.

"Lord, help me to be a faithful steward—a servant who is responsible for investing Your resources. Show me how to identify my greatest talents and abilities and use them to bless others, pointing them to You. Amen."

WHO AM I?

I am a praying person.

THINK ABOUT IT

Prayer is not a mystical, religious practice that can be done only by experts. In its purest form, it is merely the act of having a conversation with God. And what is a typical conversation? It is both talking AND listening. Where do you go when you want to spend time alone with God? How often do you talk to Him? Though you may not hear an actual voice, how can you hear God speak to you?

READ ABOUT IT

"Let me hear of your unfailing love to me in the morning, for I am trusting you. Show me where to walk, for I have come to you in prayer." (Psalm 143:8 NLT)

"Very early in the morning, while it was still dark, Jesus got up, left the house and went off to a solitary place, where he prayed." (Mark 1:35)

HOW TO PRAY

"When you pray, don't be like the hypocrites who love to pray publicly on street corners and in the synagogues where everyone can see them. I assure you, that is all the reward they will ever get. But when you pray, go away by yourself, shut the door behind you, and pray to your Father secretly. Then your Father, who knows all secrets, will reward you.

"When you pray, don't babble on and on as people of other religions do. They think their prayers are answered only by repeating their words again and again. Don't be like them, because your Father knows exactly what you need even before you ask Him! Pray like this:

Our Father in heaven, may your name be honored.
May your Kingdom come soon.
May your will be done here on earth, just as it is in heaven.
Give us our food for today, and forgive us our sins,
    just as we have forgiven those who have sinned against us.
And don't let us yield to temptation,
    but deliver us from the evil one."

(Matthew 6:5–13 NLT)

WRITE ABOUT IT

Another way to pray is to write God a letter. Write a prayer down and then spend some time reading Matthew chapter 6. As you read, "listen" for God's Word to speak to you. Pray about what you "hear."

1 Shout for joy to the LORD, all the earth.
2 Worship the LORD with gladness;
   come before him with joyful songs.
3 Know that the LORD is God.
   It is he who made us, and we are his;
   we are his people, the sheep of his pasture.

4 Enter his gates with thanksgiving
   and his courts with praise;
   give thanks to him and praise his name.
5 For the LORD is good and his love endures forever;
   his faithfulness continues through all generations.

PSALM **100**

Too often church is thought of as a passive experience where the congregation does nothing but sit and listen to the pastor, the choir, and the person who reads the Scripture passages. Perhaps this is why people often say church is "boring." Well, the truth is that worship—regardless of the style, the order, or the length of the service—is a celebration of the life, the death, the resurrection, and the glorious return of Christ our Savior. Keep this incredible fact in mind when you go to church this Sunday, and let your heart and mind and voice respond accordingly.

FOR THE LORD IS **GOOD** AND HIS **LOVE** ENDURES FOREVER

WHO AM I?

I am a changing person in a constantly changing world.

THINK ABOUT IT

How do you usually react when things change, go wrong, or do not work out? What can you do to improve your reactions when facing disappointments or difficult situations?

READ ABOUT IT

"For our present troubles are quite small and won't last very long. Yet they produce for us an immeasurably great glory that will last forever! So we don't look at the troubles we can see right now; rather, we look forward to what we have not yet seen. For the troubles we see will soon be over, but the joys to come will last forever." (2 Corinthians 4:17–18 NLT)

THE CHALLENGE OF CHANGE

From the moment of conception, we never stop changing. We were designed to be always growing, learning, and aging. And if that were not enough, God has made the universe and everything in it so that it is always in a state of change. Our galaxy is expanding, our solar system is in constant motion, seasons change, rivers cut canyons through mountains, acorns grow into towering oaks, babies are born, old people die, caterpillars morph into butterflies—all changes ordained by God to move creation in a direction of His choosing.

Relax. Take it easy. Don't get so worked up. It's sure easy to act cool and give advice when you're not the one facing a tough situation or difficult decision. It's not so simple, however, when you're in the hot seat and are on the receiving end of such "great" wisdom. There are two things you should never forget when you're faced with a monumental upheaval in your life: (1) No problem or transition lasts forever, and (2) things always seem worse than they really are when you're the one affected. Oh yeah, and there's something else you should never forget: When you're a Christian, no matter what the circumstances are, God will always listen to you, He will always guide you, and He will never abandon you.

WRITE ABOUT IT

List three positive changes that you have experienced. How have they made your life different?
Now list three negative changes. How have they affected your life?

I am responsible for how I spend my days.

THINK ABOUT IT

What part of your day do you enjoy the most? What part of your day could you use more effectively?

READ ABOUT IT

**"Teach us to make the most of our time, so that we may grow in wisdom."
(Psalm 90:12 NLT)**

There is nothing that can slip away faster than time (unless it's money). Each day that you wake up and roll out of bed is a priceless gift. How you use that gift is up to you.

86,400

Imagine if you had a rich uncle who gave you a bank account into which $86,400 was deposited each day. You could spend the money any way you wanted but, at the end of the day, whatever you didn't spend would be deleted from the account. That money would be gone forever. But don't worry—the next day, you'd have another $86,400 waiting for you—as long as your rich uncle chose to keep the cash flowing.

Dream on! you're thinking. But wait! Every single one of us has 86,400 seconds in each new 24-hour day. All we have to do is choose how to use them. We can invest them or waste them, but we never get any of them back. And we have no guarantee that we will have another 86,400 the next day.

WRITE ABOUT IT

List five ways you waste time.

List five ways you can use time wisely.

WHO AM I?

I am a visionary.

THINK ABOUT IT

Where do you see yourself in ten years . . . twenty years . . . thirty years? How do you plan to make a difference in the world as your life unfolds?

READ ABOUT IT

"For I know the plans I have for you," says the LORD. "They are plans for good and not for disaster, to give you a future and a hope." (Jeremiah 29:11 NLT)

Just as there are some who get in their car and drive aimlessly to a place they've never been, so there are many who embark on life's path without a clue of where they're headed. In both cases the smartest thing to do is take along a map. And read it. You can buy a road map at any gas station. But the guide for life's journey can only be found in the pages of God's Word.

THINK OF THE END IN THE BEGINNING

Nehemiah was truly a man of vision. He and his fellow Jews desired to rebuild the wall around Jerusalem. Fifty-two days later, the wall was rebuilt. Even more amazing was the fact that the workers had to fend off their enemies while they were building. Read about the rebuilding in Nehemiah chapters 2–7.

WRITE ABOUT IT

What are some goals you have for the next year?

Spiritual Life:

Relationships:

Money:

School:

What about the next five years?

Spiritual Life:

Relationships:

Money:

Career:

It's a loud, loud world.

Cars. Music. Teachers. Television. The first period bell. Your parents (sometimes). Your friends (always). Together it's all just a deafening roar. It's little wonder you can't hear yourself think sometimes, let alone pay close attention to what's going on in the world.

Because audible distractions are inescapable, many public speakers (pastors, stage actors, lecturers, etc.) have learned a clever technique to recapture an audience's attention when they become preoccupied with noises like a mower outside or people talking in the hallway. Believe it or not, they start talking softer and softer—sometimes, in fact, lowering their voices to a near whisper. The reason it works (and it does work—try it sometime when you're speaking publicly!) is that the speaker has, in a very gentle way, forced his or her listeners to pay closer attention.

It's funny, then, when people say that God never answers their prayers. They claim that since He never speaks to them, He either isn't listening or doesn't care. The truth is that God speaks to His children every moment of every day. Sure, He's not up on a cloud shouting down at us or throwing lightning bolts inches from our feet. But that's not how a loving God communicates. Instead, He shows us His grandeur through the beauty of creation; He tells us how much He loves us by showering us with countless great and small blessings, and He guides our thoughts and actions through His holy Word and by the indwelling presence of His Holy Spirit.

Remember the three simple rules you learned for crossing the street when you were little?

Stop. Look. Listen.

It's not a very complicated plan, but it always works. Now that you're much older and much, much wiser (not to mention the fact that you're a living example of the wisdom behind the "three-step intersection navigation" formula), try applying the same steps to your daily walk with the Lord. You'll be amazed at all the wonderful things He has to share with you!

THE HEAVENS DECLARE THE GLORY OF GOD;
THE SKIES PROCLAIM THE WORK OF HIS HANDS.

PSALM 19

1 The heavens declare the glory of God; the skies proclaim the work of his hands.
2 Day after day they pour forth speech; night after night they display knowledge.
3 There is no speech or language where their voice is not heard.
4 Their voice goes out into all the earth, their words to the ends of the world.

  In the heavens he has pitched a tent for the sun,
5 which is like a bridegroom coming forth from his pavilion,
  like a champion rejoicing to run his course.
6 It rises at one end of the heavens and makes its circuit to the other;
  nothing is hidden from its heat.

7 The law of the LORD is perfect, reviving the soul.
  The statutes of the LORD are trustworthy, making wise the simple.
8 The precepts of the LORD are right, giving joy to the heart.
  The commands of the LORD are radiant, giving light to the eyes.
9 The fear of the LORD is pure, enduring forever.
  The ordinances of the LORD are sure and altogether righteous.
10 They are more precious than gold, than much pure gold;
  they are sweeter than honey, than honey from the comb.
11 By them is your servant warned; in keeping them
  there is great reward.

12 Who can discern his errors? Forgive my hidden faults.
13 Keep your servant also from willful sins; may they not rule over me.
  Then will I be blameless, innocent of great transgression.

14 May the words of my mouth and the meditation of my heart
  be pleasing in your sight, O LORD, my Rock and my Redeemer.

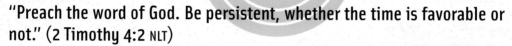

WHO AM I?

I am a witness.

THINK ABOUT IT

When have you shared the good news of Jesus Christ with others? How far are you prepared to go to share the gospel?

READ ABOUT IT

"Preach the word of God. Be persistent, whether the time is favorable or not." (2 Timothy 4:2 NLT)

"You are already clean because of the word I have spoken to you. Remain in me, and I will remain in you. . . . You did not choose me, but I chose you and appointed you to go and bear fruit—fruit that will last. (John 15:3–4, 16)

THE COURAGE OF STEPHEN

Stephen was a bold witness for Christ who stood up against fierce opposition, boldly proclaiming the truth. With God's help, he faithfully delivered the gospel message and, as a result, paid the ultimate price. Read about him in Acts chapters 6–7.

Let's face it; it's not easy to share your faith. Especially when everyone is telling you that there's no right or wrong way to believe and that to say otherwise is both ignorant and intolerant. When the apostle Paul wrote his second letter to Timothy, he understood all too well the challenges Christians face. Remember that this was a guy who had been beaten and thrown into prison for preaching the gospel. Yet he knew that, regardless of the problems he faced, nothing was more important than sharing the message of salvation with a world that so desperately needed it. The world needs the same message today! Ask the Lord, through the mighty power of His Holy Spirit, to give you the wisdom and courage you'll need to become a light shining in the darkness.

WRITE ABOUT IT

Write your testimony (the story of how Jesus has changed your life). See if you can make it short enough to fit on this page, and easy enough to retell from memory.

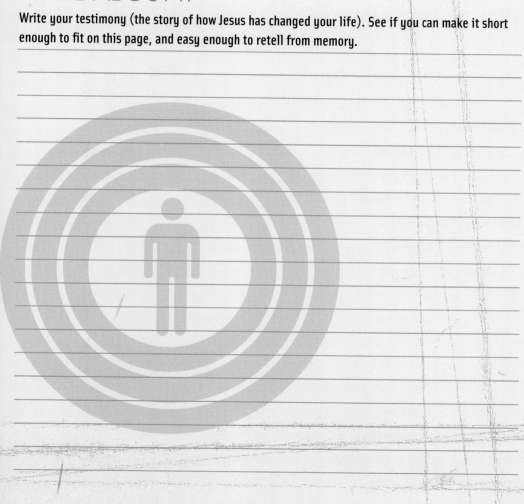

This is what the LORD says:

Cursed are those who put their trust in mere humans and turn their hearts away from the LORD. They are like stunted shrubs in the desert, with no hope for the future. They will live in the barren wilderness, on the salty flats where no one lives.

But blessed are those who trust in the LORD and have made the LORD their hope and confidence.

They are like trees planted along a riverbank, with roots that reach deep into the water. Such trees are not bothered by the heat or worried by long months of drought. Their leaves stay green, and they go right on producing delicious fruit.

WHO AM I?

I am an eternal being.

THINK ABOUT IT

The end of your life on earth is not the end of your life. *God designed you to live forever!* Death is merely a doorway you must pass through to begin living the rest of your life. Each day is like going to school; you're being prepared for *real life*. That means that everything you do today matters—it will matter forever. Since you will live forever, then you are already living in eternity! Where will you be spending the rest of your life after you "graduate" from earth?

READ ABOUT IT

"We are citizens of heaven, where the Lord Jesus Christ lives. And we are eagerly waiting for him to return as our Savior. He will take these weak mortal bodies of ours and change them into glorious bodies like his own, using the same mighty power that he will use to conquer everything, everywhere." (Philippians 3:20–21 NLT)

ETERNITY

Imagine you have a string so long that it reaches to the moon and back. Then imagine a grain of pepper on that string. The ultralong string represents eternity, and the tiny black speck on that string represents your life span here on earth. Can you see how much more important your eternal life is than the tiny pleasures, problems, and desires of this life?

Jesus reminds us, "Do not store up for yourselves treasures on earth, where moth and rust destroy, and where thieves break in and steal. But store up for yourselves treasures in heaven, where moth and rust do not destroy, and where thieves do not break in and steal. For where your treasure is there your heart will be also." (Matthew 6:19–21)

What would you want your friends to say about you after you die? How might you live each moment differently, if you knew your time on earth was almost over?

The same God who made heaven and earth made you.

Anytime you enjoy His amazing creation, you will find yourself worshiping Him! You can worship God anytime, anywhere. Make a habit of praising Him every time you look at something beautiful. He delights in our praise! True worship is enjoying God and expressing that joy.

As you look at this beautiful scene, listen to what God has to say to you about Himself. Write down some words of praise to this mighty, awesome, wonderful Creator we call our heavenly Father.

HOW WILL I BE REMEMBERED AFTER I'M GONE? WHAT WILL BE MY LEGACY? WHAT KIND OF DIFFERENCE WILL MY LIFE MAKE IN THIS WORLD, IN HEAVEN, AND IN THE LIVES OF THOSE CLOSE TO ME?

Jesus said, "There was a certain rich man who was splendidly clothed and who lived each day in luxury. At his door lay a diseased beggar named Lazarus. As Lazarus lay there longing for scraps from the rich man's table, the dogs would come and lick his open sores. Finally, the beggar died and was carried by the angels to be with Abraham. The rich man also died and was buried, and his soul went to the place of the dead. There, in torment, he saw Lazarus in the far distance with Abraham.

"The rich man shouted, 'Father Abraham, have some pity! Send Lazarus over here to dip the tip of his finger in water and cool my tongue, because I am in anguish in these flames.'

"But Abraham said to him, 'Son, remember that during your lifetime you had everything you wanted, and Lazarus had nothing. So now he is here being comforted, and you are in anguish. And besides, there is a great chasm separating us. Anyone who wanted to cross over to you from here is stopped at its edge, and no one there can cross over to us.'

"Then the rich man said, 'Please, Father Abraham, send him to my father's home. For I have five brothers, and I want him to warn them about this place of torment so they won't have to come here when they die.'

"But Abraham said, 'Moses and the prophets have warned them. Your brothers can read their writings anytime they want to.

"The rich man replied, 'No, Father Abraham! But if someone is sent to them from the dead, then they will turn from their sins.'

"But Abraham said, 'If they won't listen to Moses and the prophets, they won't listen even if someone rises from the dead.'"

(Luke 16:19–31 NLT)

Will I be remembered as someone
who served and cared for others,
who listened to and lived by God's Word,
who freely shared God's love and resources,
OR will I be remembered as someone
who took care of myself and ignored the needs of others,
who didn't listen to and live by God's Word,
who refused to share God's love and resources?

"Lord, help me to live my life with an eternal perspective. May my choices lead me and many others toward heaven. Please make my life significant, so that when my time on earth is finished, I will be remembered as one who lived life to the fullest and helped others to do the same. Amen."

WHO AM I?

I am God's beloved (and unfinished) work of art!

THINK ABOUT IT

Now that you've gone through this book and spent time talking to and listening to God, think about the many brush strokes of your personality, experience, knowledge, talents, appearance, faith, and character which make up the work of art called "you." This is who you are so far!

Use this last journaling space to summarize who you are on this day in your life's history. Put a date on it, because it will be interesting to see how much more you have become even a year after you've written this! You are a work in progress, and you will keep becoming who you are for the rest of your life!

Date: _____ A BRIEF SUMMARY OF WHO I AM AT THIS POINT IN MY LIFE:

_____

_____

_____

_____

_____

_____

_____

_____

_____

_____

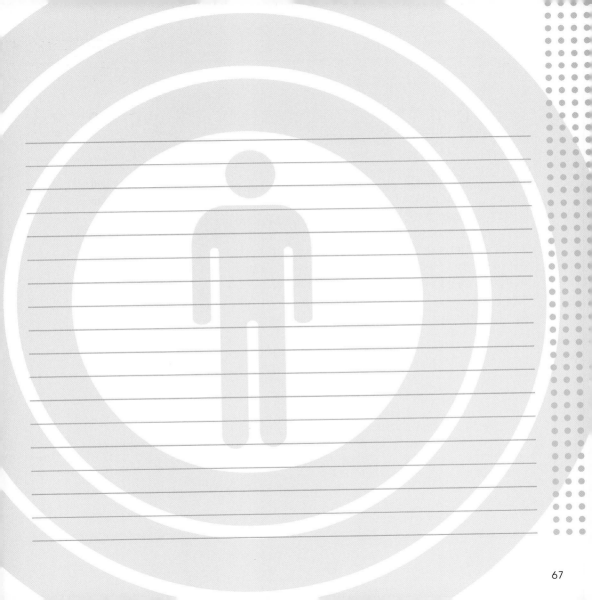

About the Authors

Matthew A. Price is a writer, publisher, and marketing consultant. He is the author or coauthor of nearly thirty books, including The Story of Christianity, a best-selling reference work that has been translated into five languages and has sold more than 250,000 copies. Matthew's background with youth-oriented projects includes the development of The EDGE, a teen devotional Bible, The Jubilee Family Illustrated Bible, and the series Squeaky Sneaker Books. He has also contributed articles for On Track and Movin' On. Matthew and his wife, Jeanie, live in Brentwood, Tennessee, with their five children.

Joel Anderson is a designer, painter, photographer, and author. He is co-owner of Anderson Thomas Design, Inc., a nationally recognized graphic design firm in Nashville. He has garnered an Emmy Award for his design work on a CBS children's show, a Dove Award for Best Album Cover of the Year, and several other awards for product design aimed at young people. Joel has designed and created numerous books, magazines, and pop-culture products for the music, publishing, and entertainment industries. He has authored or coauthored eleven books, which he also designed and illustrated. Joel enjoys painting, gardening, and family fun with his wife and four children.

More poetry for your soul . . .

A BOOK WITH ANSWERS TO
THE QUESTIONS YOU'RE ASKING

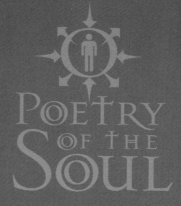

POETRY
OF THE
SOUL